THE ROYAL HORTICULTURAL SOCIETY

— DIARY —

1995

Paintings by LILIAN SNELLING

FRANCES LINCOLN

FRANCES LINCOLN LIMITED

4 TORRIANO MEWS, TORRIANO AVENUE, LONDON NW5 2RZ

THE ROYAL HORTICULTURAL SOCIETY DIARY 1995

COPYRIGHT © FRANCES LINCOLN LIMITED 1994

ILLUSTRATION COPYRIGHT © THE ROYAL HORTICULTURAL SOCIETY 1994

ASTRONOMICAL INFORMATION REPRODUCED, WITH PERMISSION, FROM DATA PRODUCED BY HM NAUTICAL
ALMANAC OFFICE, COPYRIGHT © SCIENCE AND ENGINEERING RESEARCH COUNCIL

DESIGN BY DAVID FORDHAM

BRITISH LIBRARY CATALOGUING IN PUBLICATION DATA.

A CATALOGUE RECORD FOR THIS BOOK IS AVAILABLE FROM THE BRITISH LIBRARY.

ISBN 0-7112-0826-3

TYPESET BY SX COMPOSING

PRINTED IN HONG KONG

FIRST FRANCES LINCOLN EDITION: JULY 1994

80-501-1

RHS FLOWER SHOWS 1995

All shows feature a wide range of floral exhibits staged by the nursery trade, with associated competitions reflecting seasonal changes, and horticultural sundries.

With the exception of the shows at Harrogate, Malvern, Chelsea, Birmingham, Hampton Court and Wisley, all RHS Flower Shows will be held in one or both of the Society's Horticultural Halls in Greycoat Street and Vincent Square, Westminster, London SW1.

The dates are correct at time of going to press. Any amendments or alterations will be notified in the Society's journal, *The Garden*. Up-to-date information on the Society's Flower Shows is available on the RHS 24-hour information line, 071 828 1744.

YEAR PLANNER

1995

January
M	T	W	T	F	S	S
						1
2	3	4	5	6	7	8
9	10	11	12	13	14	15
16	17	18	19	20	21	22
23	24	25	26	27	28	29
30	31					

February
M	T	W	T	F	S	S
		1	2	3	4	5
6	7	8	9	10	11	12
13	14	15	16	17	18	19
20	21	22	23	24	25	26
27	28					

March
M	T	W	T	F	S	S
		1	2	3	4	5
6	7	8	9	10	11	12
13	14	15	16	17	18	19
20	21	22	23	24	25	26
27	28	29	30	31		

April
M	T	W	T	F	S	S
					1	2
3	4	5	6	7	8	9
10	11	12	13	14	15	16
17	18	19	20	21	22	23
24	25	26	27	28	29	30

May
M	T	W	T	F	S	S
1	2	3	4	5	6	7
8	9	10	11	12	13	14
15	16	17	18	19	20	21
22	23	24	25	26	27	28
29	30	31				

June
M	T	W	T	F	S	S
			1	2	3	4
5	6	7	8	9	10	11
12	13	14	15	16	17	18
19	20	21	22	23	24	25
26	27	28	29	30		

July
M	T	W	T	F	S	S
					1	2
3	4	5	6	7	8	9
10	11	12	13	14	15	16
17	18	19	20	21	22	23
24	25	26	27	28	29	30
31						

August
M	T	W	T	F	S	S
1	2	3	4	5	6
7	8	9	10	11	12	13
14	15	16	17	18	19	20
21	22	23	24	25	26	27
28	29	30	31			

September
M	T	W	T	F	S	S
				1	2	3
4	5	6	7	8	9	10
11	12	13	14	15	16	17
18	19	20	21	22	23	24
25	26	27	28	29	30	

October
M	T	W	T	F	S	S
						1
2	3	4	5	6	7	8
9	10	11	12	13	14	15
16	17	18	19	20	21	22
23	24	25	26	27	28	29
30	31					

November
M	T	W	T	F	S	S
		1	2	3	4	5
6	7	8	9	10	11	12
13	14	15	16	17	18	19
20	21	22	23	24	25	26
27	28	29	30			

December
M	T	W	T	F	S	S
				1	2	3
4	5	6	7	8	9	10
11	12	13	14	15	16	17
18	19	20	21	22	23	24
25	26	27	28	29	30	31

1996

January
M	T	W	T	F	S	S
1	2	3	4	5	6	7
8	9	10	11	12	13	14
15	16	17	18	19	20	21
22	23	24	25	26	27	28
29	30	31				

February
M	T	W	T	F	S	S
			1	2	3	4
5	6	7	8	9	10	11
12	13	14	15	16	17	18
19	20	21	22	23	24	25
26	27	28	29			

March
M	T	W	T	F	S	S
				1	2	3
4	5	6	7	8	9	10
11	12	13	14	15	16	17
18	19	20	21	22	23	24
25	26	27	28	29	30	31

April
M	T	W	T	F	S	S
1	2	3	4	5	6	7
8	9	10	11	12	13	14
15	16	17	18	19	20	21
22	23	24	25	26	27	28
29	30					

May
M	T	W	T	F	S	S
		1	2	3	4	5
6	7	8	9	10	11	12
13	14	15	16	17	18	19
20	21	22	23	24	25	26
27	28	29	30	31		

June
M	T	W	T	F	S	S
					1	2
3	4	5	6	7	8	9
10	11	12	13	14	15	16
17	18	19	20	21	22	23
24	25	26	27	28	29	30

July
M	T	W	T	F	S	S
1	2	3	4	5	6	7
8	9	10	11	12	13	14
15	16	17	18	19	20	21
22	23	24	25	26	27	28
29	30	31				

August
M	T	W	T	F	S	S
			1	2	3	4
5	6	7	8	9	10	11
12	13	14	15	16	17	18
19	20	21	22	23	24	25
26	27	28	29	30	31	

September
M	T	W	T	F	S	S
						1
2	3	4	5	6	7	8
9	10	11	12	13	14	15
16	17	18	19	20	21	22
23	24	25	26	27	28	29
30						

October
M	T	W	T	F	S	S
	1	2	3	4	5	6
7	8	9	10	11	12	13
14	15	16	17	18	19	20
21	22	23	24	25	26	27
28	29	30	31			

November
M	T	W	T	F	S	S
				1	2	3
4	5	6	7	8	9	10
11	12	13	14	15	16	17
18	19	20	21	22	23	24
25	26	27	28	29	30	

December
M	T	W	T	F	S	S
						1
2	3	4	5	6	7	8
9	10	11	12	13	14	15
16	17	18	19	20	21	22
23	24	25	26	27	28	29
30	31					

○ Full Moon
◑ First Quarter
● New Moon
◐ Last Quarter

LILIAN SNELLING
1879-1972

'HER WORK AS A BOTANICAL ARTIST IS WITHOUT LIVING PEER [and] as a botanical illustrator and technician her work materially eclipses that of Redouté,' wrote the distinguished botanist Dr George Lawrence, on hearing of the death of Lilian Snelling.

Lilian Snelling was born in St Mary Cray in Kent to a well-known family of millers, who at one time owned the local brewery. The youngest of the family, she spent most of her life in St Mary Cray, living with her three other unmarried sisters in Spring Hall, the family home. The drawings in this volume are her earliest surviving work: we are seeing her at the very beginning of her career. Most of the locations noted here are the fields and hedgerows of Kent around St Mary Cray and nearby Tunbridge Wells. The drawings are arranged chronologically: the earliest is dated 22 May 1900, and the last 27 July 1905, but the majority were painted in 1900 and 1901. The composite pictures, which formed the sketchbook she kept in her early twenties, were not completed at single sittings; often, she would return to a partially finished drawing and add further plants. Most of the plants are British wild flowers; a few are garden varieties.

After studying art and lithography at the Royal College of Art in London, she worked as the protégée of the arboriculturist and plant hunter Henry John Elwes (1846-1922), painting plants that grew in his garden at Colesbourne in Gloucestershire. (When Arthur Grove published two supplements to Elwes' *Monograph of the Genus Lilium*, 1933-1940, it was to Lilian Snelling that he turned for the magnificent illustrations, which are regarded as her masterpiece.)

From 1916 to 1921 Lilian Snelling worked at the Royal Botanic Garden, Edinburgh, under the guidance of the Keeper, Sir Isaac Bayley Balfour, and it was there that she developed the meticulous style that was to stand her in such good stead on *Curtis's Botanical Magazine*, which had been purchased by the Royal Horticultural Society in 1921.

In 1922 she was hired as the magazine's principal illustrator and lithographer and, over a period of thirty years, she made over 740 plates, an achievement that put her at the forefront of her art. Volume 169 was dedicated to her, with praise for her 'remarkable delicacy of accurate outlines, brilliancy of colour and intricate gradation of tone'.

Lilian Snelling retired from the *Botanical Magazine* in 1952. She was awarded the MBE in 1954 and the Victoria Medal of Honour, the Royal Horticultural Society's highest award, in 1955. The last of the sisters to survive, she died at the age of ninety-three.

The flowering of Lilian Snelling's mature style formed the outstanding model for the British botanical artists of the last half-century. The drawings in this volume, published for the first time, show a hitherto unknown phase of her career, giving the opportunity to see her talent in the bud.

BRENT ELLIOTT
The Royal Horticultural Society

Bitter vetch, *Lathyrus linifolius* var. *montanus* (I); germander speedwell, *Veronica chamaedrys* (II); lousewort or dwarf red rattle, *Pedicularis sylvatica* (III); tormentil, *Potentilla erecta* (IV); pale dog violet, *Viola lactea* (V); bugle, *Ajuga reptans* (VI); herb Robert, *Geranium robertianum* (VII); creeping cinquefoil, *Potentilla reptans* (VIII); ground ivy, *Glechoma hederacea* (IX); and common vetch, *Vicia sativa* (X)

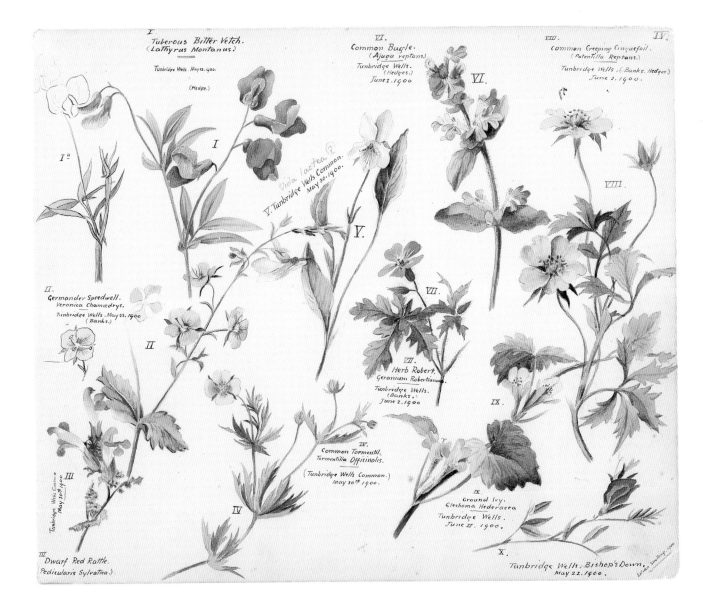

I.
Tuberous Bitter Vetch.
(Lathyrus Montanus.)

Tunbridge Wells. May 22. 1900.

(Hedge.)

I.ª

I.

VI.
Common Bugle.
(Ajuga reptans.)
Tunbridge Wells.
(Hedges.)
June 1. 1900

VI.

VIII.
Common Creeping Cinquefoil
(Potentilla Reptans.)

Tunbridge Wells. (. Banks. Hedges.)
June 2. 1900.

VIII.

Viola lactea ?
V. Tunbridge Wells Common.
May 30. 1900.

V.

II.
Germander Speedwell.
Veronica Chamædrys.
Tunbridge Wells . May 22. 1900
(Banks.)

II.

VII.

VII.
Herb Robert.
Geranium Robertianum.
Tunbridge Wells.
(Banks.)
June 2. 1900.

III
Tunbridge Wells Common
May 30ᵗʰ 1900

IX.

IV.
Common Tormentil.
Tormentilla Officinalis.

(Tunbridge Wells Common.)
May 30ᵗʰ 1900.

IV.

IX
Ground Ivy.
Glechoma Hederacea
Tunbridge Wells.
June II. 1900.

X.

III
Dwarf Red Rattle.
(Pedicularis Sylvatica.)

Tunbridge Wells. Bishop's Down.
May 22. 1900.

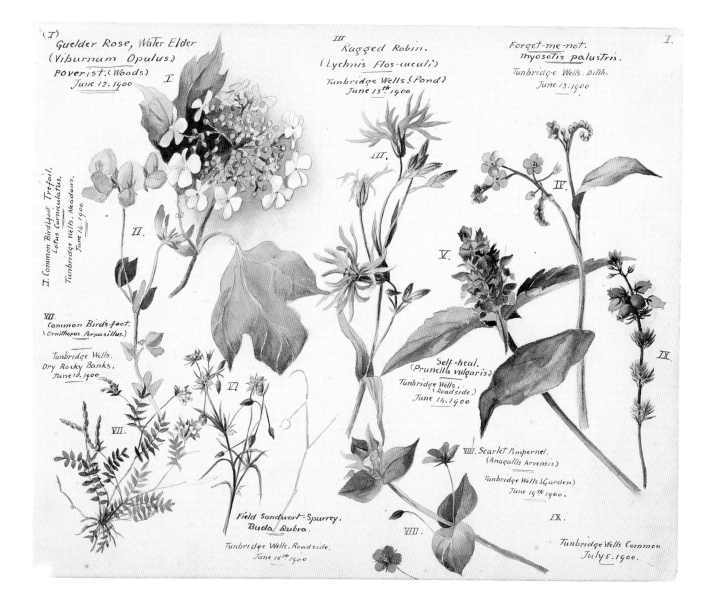

(I)

Guelder Rose, Water Elder
(Viburnum Opulus)
Poverist. (Woods)
June 12. 1900

I.

III
Ragged Robin.
(Lychnis Flos-cuculi)
Tunbridge Wells. (Pond)
June 13th 1900

III.

Forget-me-not.
myosotis palustris.
Tunbridge Wells. Ditch.
June 13. 1900

I.

II. Common Birdsfoot Trefoil.
Lotus Corniculatus.
Tunbridge Wells. Meadows.
June 14. 1900

II.

IV.

V.

VII. Common Birds-foot.
(Ornithopus Perpusillus.)
Tunbridge Wells.
Dry Rocky Banks.
June 18. 1900

VII.

VI.

Self-heal.
(Prunella vulgaris)
Tunbridge Wells.
(Roadside.)
June 14. 1900

IX.

Field Sandwort=Spurrey.
Buda Rubra.
Tunbridge Wells. Roadside.
June 15th 1900

VIII. Scarlet Pimpernel.
(Anagallis Arvensis.)
Tunbridge Wells. (Garden)
June 19th 1900

VIII.

IX.

Tunbridge Wells Common
July 5. 1900.

DECEMBER *1994* / JANUARY *1995*

26 Monday — BOXING DAY, ST. STEPHEN'S DAY HOLIDAY, UK (INC. SCOTLAND), REPUBLIC OF IRELAND, CANADA, USA, AUSTRALIA AND NEW ZEALAND

27 Tuesday — HOLIDAY, UK (INC. SCOTLAND), REPUBLIC OF IRELAND, CANADA, AUSTRALIA AND NEW ZEALAND

28 Wednesday

29 Thursday

30 Friday

31 Saturday

1 Sunday ● — NEW YEAR'S DAY

Guelder-rose, *Viburnum opulus* (I); common bird's-foot trefoil, *Lotus corniculatus* (II); ragged Robin, *Lychnis flos-cuculi* (III); water forget-me-not, *Myosotis scorpioides* (IV); self-heal, *Prunella vulgaris* (V); sand spurrey, *Spergularia rubra* (VI); bird's-foot, *Ornithopus perpusillus* (VII); scarlet pimpernel, *Anagallis arvensis* (VIII); and bell heather, *Erica cinerea* (IX)

JANUARY *1995*

2 Monday HOLIDAY, UK (INC. SCOTLAND), REPUBLIC
OF IRELAND, CANADA, USA,
AUSTRALIA AND NEW ZEALAND

6 Friday EPIPHANY

3 Tuesday HOLIDAY, SCOTLAND AND NEW ZEALAND

7 Saturday

4 Wednesday

8 Sunday ◑

5 Thursday

Common milkwort, *Polygala vulgaris* (I); yellow pim-
pernel, *Lysimachia nemorum* (II); bladder campion,
Silene vulgaris (III); a form of dog rose, *Rosa canina* (IV);
field forget-me-not, *Myosotis arvensis* (V); bush vetch,
Vicia sepium (VI); harebell, *Campanula rotundifolia*
(VII); and slender St. John's wort, *Hypericum pulchrum*
(VIII)

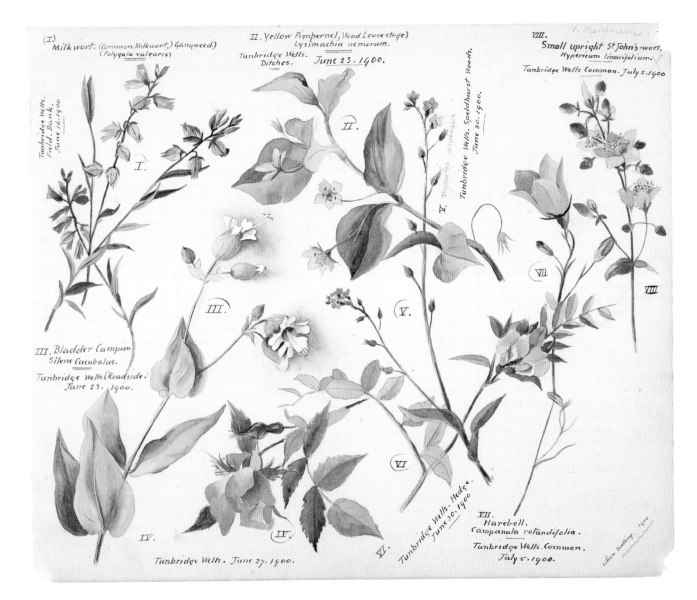

(I.)
Milk wort. (Common. Milkwort.) Gangweed.)
(Polygala vulgaris)

Tunbridge Wells.
Field. Bank.
June 16.1900.

I.

II. Yellow Pimpernel, (Wood Loose strife.)
Lysimachia nemorum.

Tunbridge Wells.
Ditches. June 23. 1900.

II.

V. myosotis arvensis

Tunbridge Wells. Speldhurst Woods.
June 30. 1900.

V.

VIII.
Small upright St John's-wort.
Hypericum linarifolium.

Tunbridge Wells Common. July 5.1900

VII.

VIII.

III.

III. Bladder Campion
Silene Cucubalus.

Tunbridge Wells (Roadside.)
June 23. 1900.

IV.

IV.

Tunbridge Wells. June 27. 1900.

VI.

VI. Tunbridge Wells. Hedge.
June 30. 1900

VII.
Harebell.
Campanula rotundifolia.

Tunbridge Wells. Common.
July 5. 1900.

Lilian Snelling. 1900

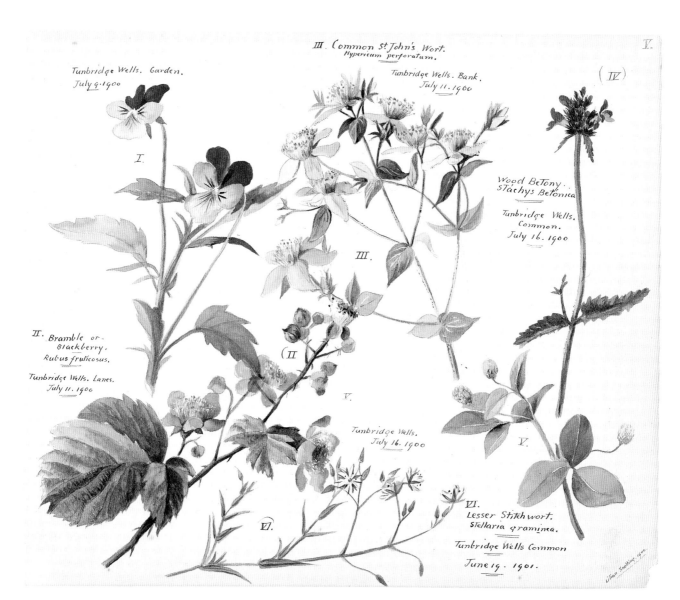

III. Common St John's Wort.
Hypericum perforatum.

V.

Tunbridge Wells. Garden.
July 9. 1900.

Tunbridge Wells. Bank.
July 11. 1900.

(IV)

I.

Wood Betony.
Stachys Betonica

Tunbridge Wells.
Common.
July 16. 1900.

III.

II. Bramble or-
Blackberry.
Rubus fruticosus.

Tunbridge Wells. Lanes.
July 11. 1900.

(II)

V.

V.

Tunbridge Wells.
July 16. 1900.

V.

VI.

VI. Lesser Stitchwort.
Stellaria graminea.

Tunbridge Wells Common

June 19. 1901.

Lilian Snelling. 1900.

JANUARY *1995*

9 Monday

10 Tuesday

11 Wednesday

12 Thursday

13 Friday

14 Saturday

15 Sunday

Wild pansy or heartsease, *Viola tricolor* (I); bramble or blackberry, *Rubus fruticosus* (II); perforate or St. John's wort, *Hypericum perforatum* (III); wood betony, *Betonica officinalis* (IV); black medick, *Medicago lupulina* (V); and lesser stitchwort, *Stellaria graminea* (VI)

JANUARY *1995*

16 Monday ○

HOLIDAY, USA
(MARTIN LUTHER KING'S BIRTHDAY)

17 Tuesday

18 Wednesday

19 Thursday

20 Friday

21 Saturday

22 Sunday

Alsike clover, *Trifolium hybridum* (opposite) and greater
bird's-foot trefoil, *Lotus pedunculatus* (right)

JANUARY *1995*

23 Monday

27 Friday

24 Tuesday ◑   RHS FLOWER SHOW

28 Saturday

25 Wednesday   RHS FLOWER SHOW

29 Sunday

26 Thursday   AUSTRALIA DAY

Honeysuckle or woodbine, *Lonicera periclymenum* (I); tufted vetch, *Vicia cracca* (II); one of the hawkweeds, *Hieracium* sp. (III); shepherd's purse, *Capsella bursa-pastoris* (IV); yarrow or milfoil, *Achillea millefolium* (V); common bird's-foot trefoil, *Lotus corniculatus* (VI); and honesty, *Lunaria annua* (VII)

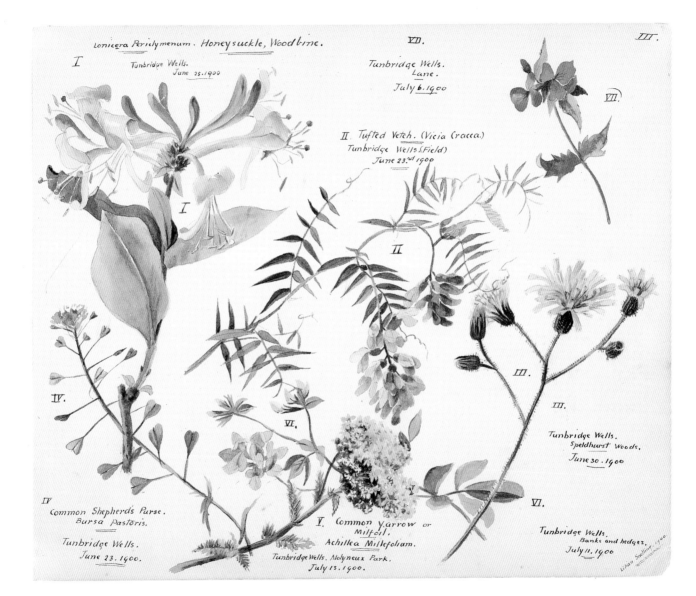

Lonicera Periclymenum. Honeysuckle, Woodbine.

VII.

III.

I.

Tunbridge Wells.
June 25.1900

Tunbridge Wells.
Lane.
July 6.1900

VII.

II. Tufted Vetch. (Vicia Cracca.)
Tunbridge Wells (Field)
June 23.rd 1900

I.

II.

III.

IV.

VI.

III.

III.
Tunbridge Wells.
Speldhurst Woods.
June 30.1900

IV. Common Shepherd's Purse.
Bursa Pastoris.

Tunbridge Wells.
June 23.1900.

V. Common Yarrow or
Milfoil.
Achillea Millefolium.

Tunbridge Wells. Molyneux Park.
July 13.1900.

VI.

Tunbridge Wells.
Banks and hedges.
July 11.1900

Lilian Snelling. 1900

I. Musk-Mallow.
Malva moschata.

Tunbridge Wells.
Molyneux Park. Field.
July 10. 1900

(I.)

IV.

III.

(II.)

Purple Foxglove.
Digitalis Purpurea.

Tunbridge Wells.
Speldhurst Woods.

July 7. 1900

VI

VII.
Common Avens or
Herb Benet.
Geum urbanum.
Cockmanning's lane.
St Mary Cray.
August 23. 1901

V.

VII

V. Yellow Rattle. or
Cock's-comb.
Rhinanthus Crista-galli.

Tunbridge Wells Common.
July 16th 1900

VI. Common Ragwort.
Senecio Jacobaea.

Tunbridge Wells. Molyneux Park. Field.

July. 10. 1900

Lilian Snelling 1900.

JANUARY/FEBRUARY *1995*

30 Monday ●

31 Tuesday   CHINESE NEW YEAR

1 Wednesday   RAMADAN BEGINS
(SUBJECT TO SIGHTING OF MOON)

2 Thursday

3 Friday

4 Saturday

5 Sunday

Musk mallow, *Malva moschata* (I); foxglove, *Digitalis purpurea* (II); possibly wild thyme, *Thymus praecox* ssp. *brittanicus* (III); possibly hairy thyme, *Thymus praecox* (IV); narrow-leaved rattle, *Rhinanthus angustifolius* (V); common ragwort, *Senecio jacobaea* (VI); and herb bennet, *Geum urbanum* (VII)

FEBRUARY *1995*

6 Monday   HOLIDAY, NEW ZEALAND (WAITANGI DAY)

7 Tuesday ◑

8 Wednesday

9 Thursday

10 Friday

11 Saturday

12 Sunday   LINCOLN'S BIRTHDAY, USA

Bittersweet, *Solanum dulcamara* (I); common centaury, *Centaurium erythraea* (II); common toadflax, *Linaria vulgaris* (III); common knapweed or hardheads, *Centaurea nigra* (IV); wood sage, *Teucrium scorodonia* (V); and common whitlow-grass, *Erophila verna* (VI)

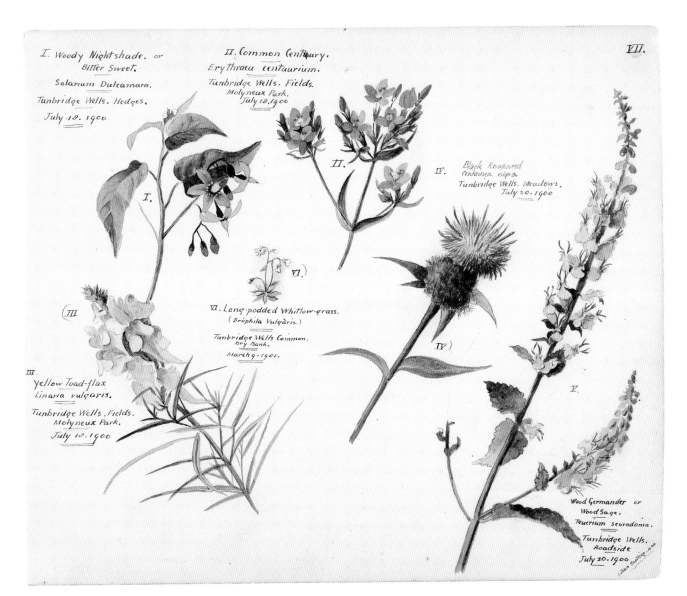

VII.

I. Woody Night shade. or
Bitter Sweet.
Solanum Dulcamara.
Tunbridge Wells. Hedges.
July 18. 1900

I.

II. Common Centaury.
Erythraea centaurium.
Tunbridge Wells. Fields.
Molyneux Park.
July 18. 1900

II.

IV. Black Knapweed
Centaurea nigra
Tunbridge Wells. Meadows.
July 20. 1900

VI.)

VI. Long-podded Whitlow-grass.
(Eróphila Vulgáris.)
Tunbridge Wells Common.
Dry Bank.
March 9. 1901.

IV.)

III.

III. Yellow Toad-flax
Linaria vulgaris.
Tunbridge Wells. Fields.
Molyneux Park.
July 18. 1900

V.

Wood Germander or
Wood Sage.
Teucrium scorodonia.
Tunbridge Wells.
Roadside
July 20. 1900

Lilian Snelling 1900

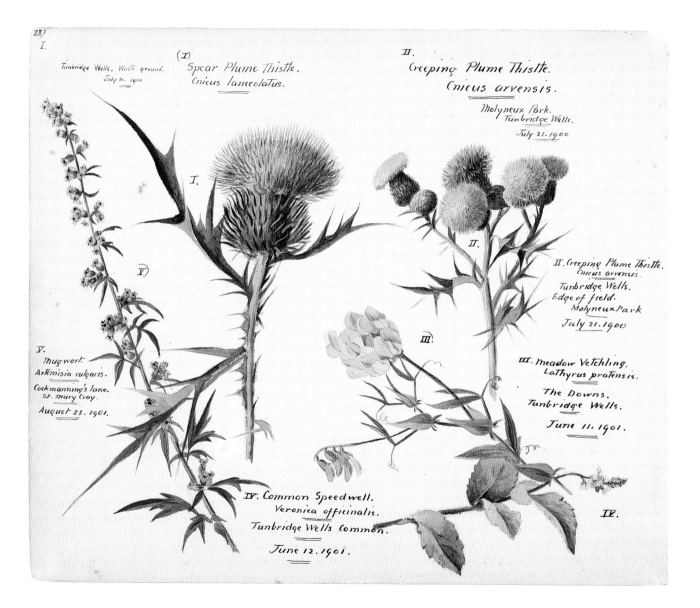

22)

I.

Tunbridge Wells. Waste ground.
July 21. 1900

(I) Spear Plume Thistle.
Cnicus lanceolatus.

II.
Creeping Plume Thistle.
Cnicus arvensis.

Molyneux Park.
Tunbridge Wells.
July 21. 1900

I.

II.

V

V. Mugwort.
Artemisia vulgaris.
Cockmanning's lane.
St. Mary Cray.
August 23. 1901.

III.

II. Creeping Plume Thistle.
Cnicus arvensis.
Tunbridge Wells.
Edge of field.
Molyneux Park
July 21. 1900

III. Meadow Vetchling.
Lathyrus pratensis.
The Downs.
Tunbridge Wells.
June 11. 1901.

IV. Common Speedwell.
Veronica officinalis.
Tunbridge Wells Common.
June 12. 1901.

IV.

13 Monday

17 Friday

14 Tuesday   ST. VALENTINE'S DAY

18 Saturday

15 Wednesday ○

19 Sunday

16 Thursday

Spear thistle, *Cirsium vulgare* (I); creeping thistle, *Cirsium arvense* (II); meadow vetchling, *Lathyrus pratensis* (III); heath speedwell, *Veronica officinalis* (IV); and mugwort, *Artemisia vulgaris* (V)

FEBRUARY *1995*

20 Monday   HOLIDAY, USA (WASHINGTON'S BIRTHDAY)

21 Tuesday   RHS FLOWER SHOW

22 Wednesday ◑   RHS FLOWER SHOW

23 Thursday

24 Friday

25 Saturday

26 Sunday

Meadow crane's-bill, *Geranium pratense* (opposite) and
yellow rattle, *Rhinanthus minor* (right)

27 Monday

3 Friday

28 Tuesday   SHROVE TUESDAY

4 Saturday

1 Wednesday ●   ASH WEDNESDAY
                          ST. DAVID'S DAY, WALES

5 Sunday

2 Thursday

Dyer's greenweed, *Genista tinctoria* (I); probably a hybrid with red campion, *Silene dioica* (II); lesser burdock, *Arctium minus* (III); probably common field speedwell, *Veronica persica* (IV); chicory, *Cichorium intybus* (V); and insipid stonecrop, *Sedum sexangulare* (VI)

XV.

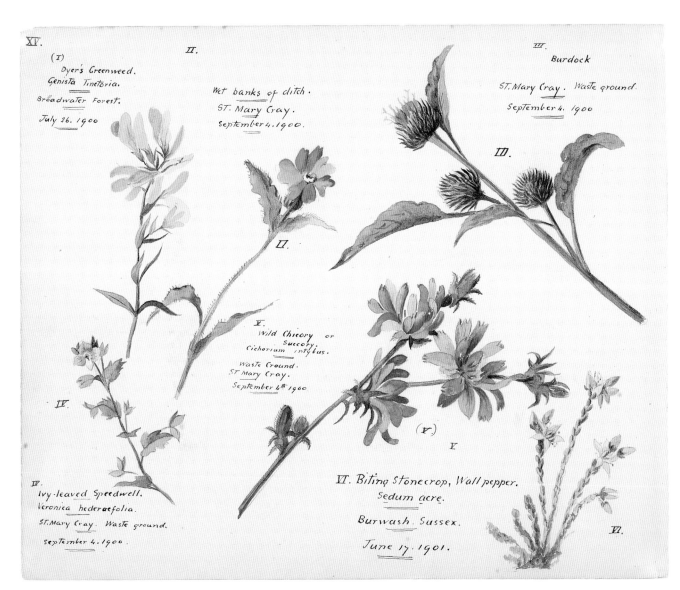

(I)
Dyer's Greenweed.
Genista Tinctoria.
Broadwater Forest.
July 26. 1900

II.
Wet banks of ditch.
ST. Mary Cray.
September 4. 1900.

II.

III.
Burdock
ST. Mary Cray. Waste ground.
September 4. 1900

III.

V.
Wild Chicory or Succory.
Cichorium intybus.
Waste Ground.
ST. Mary Cray.
September 4th 1900

IV.

IV.
Ivy-leaved Speedwell.
Veronica hederaefolia.
ST. Mary Cray. Waste ground.
September 4. 1900.

(V)

V.

VI. Biting Stonecrop, Wall pepper.
Sedum acre.
Burwash. Sussex.
June 17. 1901.

VI.

I)

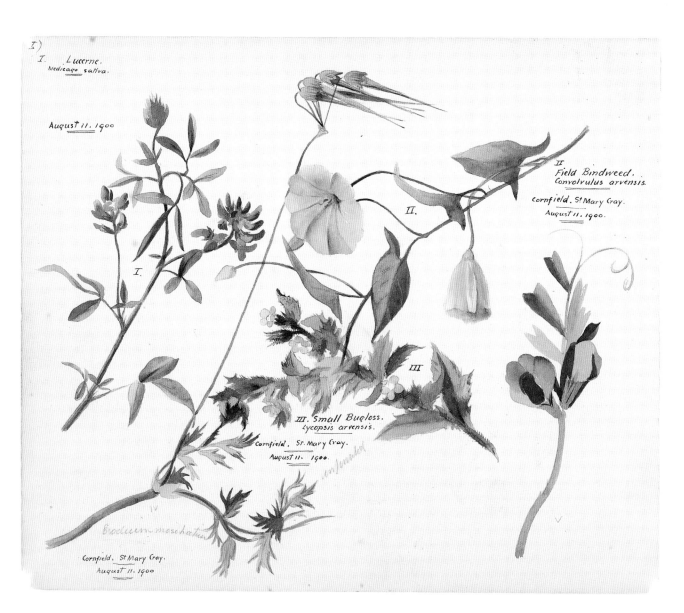

I. *Lucerne.*
Medicago sativa.

August 11. 1900

I.

II.

II *Field Bindweed.*
Convolvulus arvensis.

Cornfield. St. Mary Cray.
August 11. 1900.

III

III. *Small Bugloss.*
Lycopsis arvensis.

Cornfield. St. Mary Cray.
August 11. 1900.

IV

Erodium moschatum

V

Cornfield. St. Mary Cray.
August 11. 1900

6 Monday

10 Friday

7 Tuesday

11 Saturday   RHS ORCHID SHOW

8 Wednesday

12 Sunday   RHS ORCHID SHOW

9 Thursday ☽

Lucerne, *Medicago sativa* (I); field bindweed, *Convolvulus arvensis* (II); small bugloss, *Lycopsis arvensis* (III); musk stork's bill, *Erodium moschatum* (IV); and common vetch, *Vicia sativa* ssp. *segetalis* (V)

MARCH *1995*

13 Monday   COMMONWEALTH DAY

14 Tuesday   RHS FLOWER SHOW

15 Wednesday   RHS FLOWER SHOW

16 Thursday

17 Friday ○   ST. PATRICK'S DAY
HOLIDAY, NORTHERN IRELAND
AND REPUBLIC OF IRELAND

18 Saturday

19 Sunday

A mauve-flowered form of wild radish, *Raphanus raphanistrum* (I); white-flowered knapweed, *Centaurea scabiosa* (II); agrimony, *Agrimonia eupatoria* (III); field scabious, *Knautia arvensis* (IV); common rockrose, *Helianthemum nummularium* (V); wild mignonette, *Reseda lutea* (VI); common rest-harrow, *Ononis repens* (VII); and common sundew, *Drosera rotundifolia* (VIII)

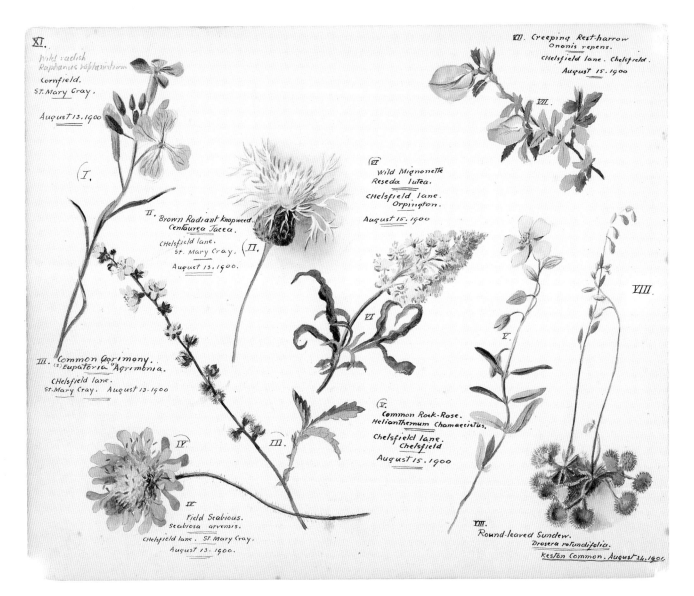

XI.

Wild radish
Raphanus raphanistrum

Cornfield.
St. Mary Cray.

August 13. 1900

(I.

II. Brown Radiant Knapweed.
Centaurea Jacea.
CHelsfield lane.
St. Mary Cray. (II.

August 13. 1900.

III. Common Agrimony.
(2) Eupatoria "Agrimonia.
CHelsfield lane.
St. Mary Cray. August 13. 1900

IV.

IV.
Field Scabious.
scabiosa arvensis.
CHelsfield lane. St. Mary Cray.
August 13. 1900.

III.

VI. Wild Mignonette
Reseda lutea.
CHelsfield lane.
Orpington.

August 15. 1900

VI.

V. Common Rock-Rose.
Helianthemum Chamaecistus.
Chelsfield lane.
Chelsfield
August 15. 1900

XII. Creeping Rest-harrow
Ononis repens.
CHelsfield lane. Chelsfield
August 15. 1900

VII.

V.

VIII.

VIII.
Round-leaved Sundew.
Drosera rotundifolia.
Keston Common. August 14. 1901.

I.
yellow Ox-eye. Corn Marigold.
Chrysanthemum Segetum.

Chelsfield lane. Cornfield.
August 27.
1900

Paul's Cray Common.
August 31. 1900

VIII.
Narrow-leaved Flax.
Linum angustifolium.

Orpington Mill (lane)
Orpington.

September 13.
1900.

VIII.

I.

V.

II.

II.
Deptford Pink.
Dianthus armeria.
Orpington Embankment.
August 31. 1900

III.

VII.

VII.
Sneezewort.
Achillea Ptarmica
Orpington Embankment.
August 31. 1900

III. Dark Mullein.
Verbascum nigrum.
Chelsfield lane. Hedge.
August 15. 1900

IV.

IV.
Common Mallow.
Malva Sylvestris.

Orpington.
Chislehurst Road.
Waste ground.

August 28th. 1900

(VI.)

(VI.)
Ling or Heather
Calluna Erica

Paul's Cray Common.

August 31. 1900

20 Monday

24 Friday

21 Tuesday   VERNAL EQUINOX

25 Saturday

22 Wednesday

26 Sunday   BRITISH SUMMER TIME BEGINS
MOTHERING SUNDAY, UK

23 Thursday ◐

Corn marigold, *Chrysanthemum segetum* (I); Deptford
pink, *Dianthus armeria* (II); dark mullein, *Verbascum
nigrum* (III); common mallow, *Malva sylvestris* (IV); bell
heather, *Erica cinerea* (V); heather or ling, *Calluna vulgaris* (VI); sneezewort, *Achillea ptarmica* (VII); and flax,
Linum usitatissimum (VIII)

MARCH/APRIL 1995

27 Monday

28 Tuesday

29 Wednesday

30 Thursday

31 Friday ●

1 Saturday

2 Sunday

Daisy, *Bellis perennis* (opposite) and wild pansy or heartsease, *Viola tricolor* (right)

APRIL *1995*

3 Monday

4 Tuesday

5 Wednesday

6 Thursday

7 Friday

8 Saturday ◑

9 Sunday   PALM SUNDAY

Henbane, *Hyoscyamus niger* (I); probably hybrid with
dewberry, *Rubus caesius* (II); marjoram, *Origanum vulgare* (III); and lady's bedstraw, *Galium verum* (IV)

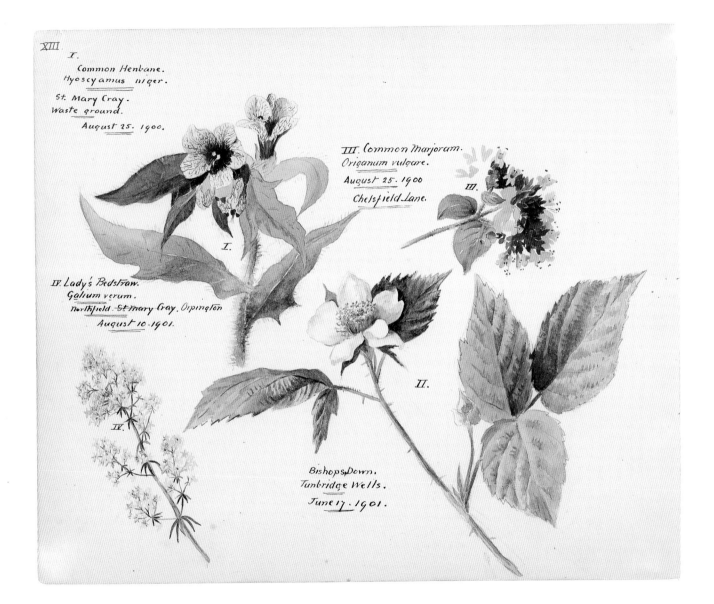

XIII

I.

Common Henbane.
Hyoscyamus niger.

St. Mary Cray.
Waste ground.

August 25. 1900.

III. Common Marjoram.
Origanum vulgare.

August 25. 1900

Chelsfield Lane.

III.

I.

IV. Lady's Bedstraw.
Galium verum.
Northfield. St Mary Cray. Orpington
August 10. 1901.

II.

IV.

Bishops Down.
Tunbridge Wells.

June 17. 1901.

XIV.

I.
Common Flea-bane.
Pulicaria Dysenterica.

Wood. Orpington.

August 31. 1900.

(I)

IV. Crosswort.
Galium Cruciata.

Burwash. Sussex.

June 17. 1901

IV)

III.
Hairy Mint.
Mentha Hirsuta.

Wet banks, of rivers.
St. Mary Cray.

August 31. 1900.

(III)

V)

II) Brown Radiant Knapweed.
Centaurea Jacea.

Crown Wood (edge).
Skeet Hill.

August 31. 1900.

II.

V.
Hedge Bedstraw.
Galium Mollugo.
Tunbridge Wells Common.

June 17. 1901.

VI.

VI. Common Hedge-mustard.
Sisymbrium officinale.

Roadside. Tunbridge Wells.

June 18. 1901.

10 Monday

14 Friday   GOOD FRIDAY

11 Tuesday   RHS FLOWER SHOW

15 Saturday ○   PASSOVER (PESACH) FIRST DAY
                                                  HOLIDAY, AUSTRALIA

12 Wednesday   RHS FLOWER SHOW

16 Sunday   EASTER DAY

13 Thursday   MAUNDY THURSDAY

Common fleabane, *Pulicaria dysenterica* (I); greater
knapweed, *Centaurea scabiosa* (II); water mint, *Mentha
aquatica* (III); crosswort, *Cruciata laevipes* (IV); hedge
bedstraw, *Galium mollugo* (V); and hedge mustard,
Sisymbrium officinale (VI)

APRIL *1995*

17 Monday

EASTER MONDAY
HOLIDAY (EXC. SCOTLAND AND USA)

18 Tuesday

19 Wednesday

20 Thursday

HARROGATE SPRING SHOW

21 Friday

PASSOVER (PESACH) SEVENTH DAY
BIRTHDAY OF QUEEN ELIZABETH II
HARROGATE SPRING SHOW

22 Saturday ◗

PASSOVER (PESACH) EIGHTH DAY
HARROGATE SPRING SHOW

23 Sunday

ST. GEORGE'S DAY, ENGLAND
HARROGATE SPRING SHOW

Coltsfoot, *Tussilago farfara* (I); common field speedwell, *Veronica persica* (II); red campion, *Silene dioica* (III); sweet violet, *Viola odorata* (IV); and pignut, *Conopodium majus* (V)

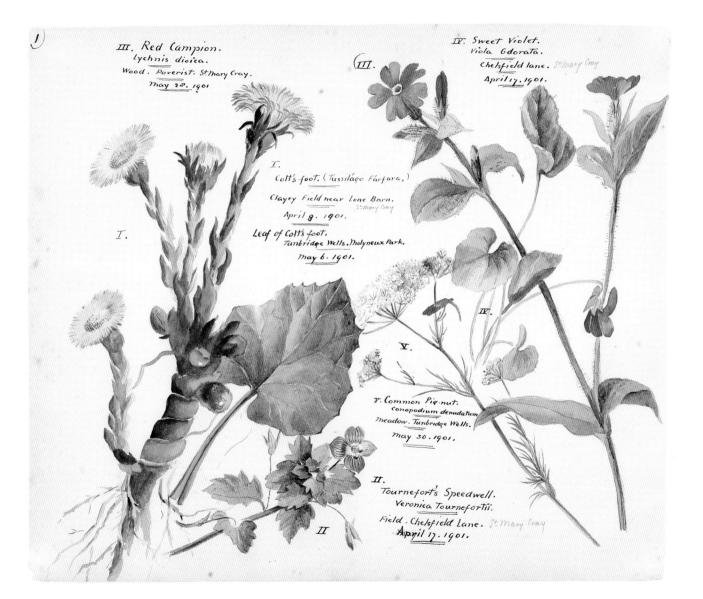

1

III. Red Campion.
Lychnis dioica.
Wood. Poverist. St Mary Cray.
May 28. 1901

IV. Sweet Violet.
Viola Odorata.
Chelsfield lane. St Mary Cray
April 17. 1901.

III.

I. Cott's-foot. (Tussilago Farfara.)
Clayey Field near Lone Barn.
St Mary Cray
April 8. 1901.
Leaf of Cott's foot.
Tunbridge Wells. Molyneux Park.
May 6. 1901.

I.

IV.

V.

V. Common Pig-nut.
Conopodium denudatum
Meadow. Tunbridge Wells.
May 30. 1901.

II.

II. Tournefort's Speedwell.
Veronica Tournefortii.
Field. Chelsfield Lane. St Mary Cray
April 17. 1901.

III.

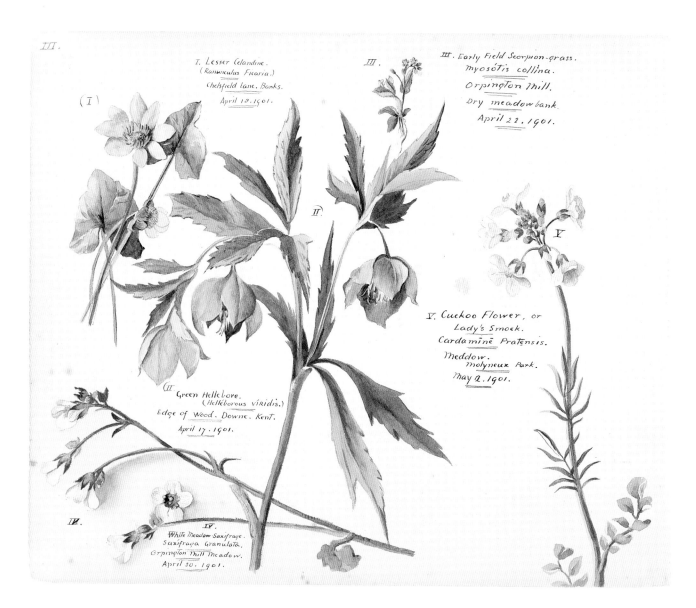

I. Lesser Celandine.
(Ranunculus Ficaria.)
Chelsfield Lane. Banks.
April 13. 1901.

(I)

III.

III. Early Field Scorpion-grass.
Myosotis collina.
Orpington Mill.
Dry meadow bank.
April 22. 1901.

II.

V.

V. Cuckoo Flower, or
Lady's Smock.
Cardaminē Pratensis.
Meadow.
Molyneux Park.
May 2. 1901.

(II) Green Hellebore.
(Helleborous viridis.)
Edge of Wood. Downe. Kent.
April 17. 1901.

IV.

IV.
White Meadow Saxifrage.
Saxifraga Granulata.
Orpington Mill Meadow.
April 30. 1901.

24 Monday

28 Friday

25 Tuesday   HOLIDAY, AUSTRALIA AND NEW ZEALAND
(ANZAC DAY)

29 Saturday ●

26 Wednesday

30 Sunday

27 Thursday

Lesser celandine, *Ranunculus ficaria* (I); green hellebore, *Helleborus viridis* (II); early forget-me-not, *Myosotis
ramosissima* (II); meadow saxifrage, *Saxifraga granulata*
(IV); and cuckoo flower or lady's smock, *Cardamine pratensis* (V)

MAY *1995*

1 Monday   MAY DAY HOLIDAY, REPUBLIC OF IRELAND
                                     SPRING HOLIDAY, SCOTLAND

2 Tuesday   RHS FLOWER SHOW

3 Wednesday   RHS FLOWER SHOW

4 Thursday

5 Friday   MALVERN SPRING GARDENING SHOW

6 Saturday   MALVERN SPRING GARDENING SHOW

7 Sunday ◑   MALVERN SPRING GARDENING SHOW

Pyramidal orchid, *Anacamptis pyramidalis* (opposite)
and wild mignonette, *Reseda lutea* (right)

MAY *1995*

8 Monday   MAY DAY HOLIDAY (VE ANNIVERSARY), UK

9 Tuesday

10 Wednesday

11 Thursday

12 Friday

13 Saturday

14 Sunday ○   MOTHER'S DAY, CANADA AND USA

Marsh marigold or kingcup, *Caltha palustris* (I); sweet violet, *Viola odorata* (II); lesser snapdragon, *Misopates orontium* (III); double-flowered creeping cinquefoil, *Potentilla reptans* (IV); red hemp-nettle, *Galeopsis angustifolia* (V); and basil thyme, *Clinopodium acinos* (VI)

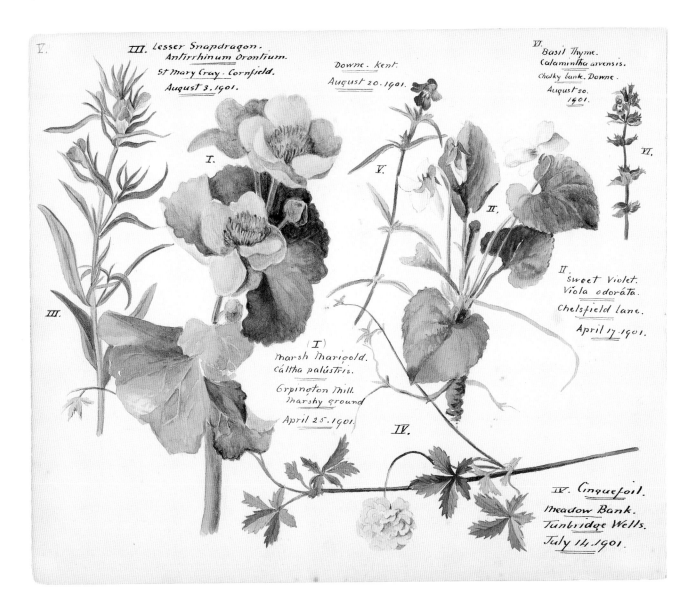

V.

III. Lesser Snapdragon.
Antirrhinum Orontium.
St Mary Cray. Cornfield.
August 3. 1901.

Downe. Kent.
August 20. 1901.

VI. Basil Thyme.
Calamintha arvensis.
Chalky bank. Downe.
August 20.
1901.

I.

V.

VI.

II.

III.

II. Sweet Violet.
Viola odoráta.
Chelsfield lane.
April 17. 1901.

(I)
Marsh Marigold.
Cáltha palústris.
Orpington Mill.
Marshy ground
April 25. 1901.

IV.

IV. Cinquefoil.
Meadow Bank.
Tunbridge Wells.
July 14. 1901.

XI.

II. Wild Hyacinth. Bluebell.
Scilla Festalis.

Wood. Burwash.

May 6. 1901.

IV. Hairy bitter Cress.
Cardamine hirsuta.

Roadside. Tunbridge Wells.

May 6. 1901.

I.

III.

I.
Primrose.
Primula Acaulis.

Woods. Burwash.

May 6. 1901.

II.

III. Cowslip. Paigle.
Primula veris.
Tunbridge Wells.
May 5. 1901.

V.

IV.

V.
Common Pellitory-of-the-wall.
Parietaria officinalis.
Cockmonning's. August 23. 1901.

15 Monday

16 Tuesday

17 Wednesday

18 Thursday

19 Friday

20 Saturday

21 Sunday ◐

Primrose, *Primula vulgaris* (I); a pinkish form of bluebell, *Hyacinthoides non-scripta* (II); cowslip, *Primula veris* (III); hairy bittercress, *Cardamine hirsuta* (IV); and pellitory of the wall, *Parietaria judaica* (V)

MAY *1995*

22 Monday   HOLIDAY, CANADA (VICTORIA DAY)

23 Tuesday   CHELSEA FLOWER SHOW

24 Wednesday   CHELSEA FLOWER SHOW

25 Thursday   ASCENSION DAY
CHELSEA FLOWER SHOW

26 Friday   CHELSEA FLOWER SHOW

27 Saturday

28 Sunday

Cat's ear, *Hypochoeris radicata* (I); a whitish form of blue-bell, *Hyacinthoides non-scripta* (II); herb Paris, *Paris quadrifolia* (III); bugle, *Ajuga reptans* (IV); and redshank, *Persicaria maculosa* (V)

V.

Common Persicaria.
Polygonum Persicaria.

Poverist. Cultivated Field.

September 2. 1901.

(II

II . Wild Hyacinth.
Scilla festalis.

Speldhurst Wood.
May 5. 1901.

(I.

III . Herb Paris, True-Love-knot.
Paris Quadrifolia.

Covert Wood. Poverist.

May 29 . 1901.

III.

V.

IV . Common Bugle.
Ajuga Reptans.

Meadow. Tunbridge Wells.

June I. 1901.

IV)

II. Common Comfrey.
Symphytum officinale.

Molyneux Park. Tunbridge Wells.
(Waste ground.)
June 18. 1901.

S. peregrinum, rather.

III. Common Broom.
Cytisus Scoparius.

Southborough Common
May 6. 1901.

II

III)

IV.

Common Yellow Melilot
Melilotus officinalis.
Waste ground. St Mary Cray.
August 1901.

29 Monday ●

SPRING HOLIDAY, UK (EXC. SCOTLAND)
MAY DAY HOLIDAY, SCOTLAND
HOLIDAY, USA (MEMORIAL DAY)

2 Friday

30 Tuesday

3 Saturday

31 Wednesday

ISLAMIC NEW YEAR
(SUBECT TO SIGHTING OF MOON)

4 Sunday

WHIT SUNDAY (PENTECOST)
JEWISH FEAST OF WEEKS (SHAVUOT)

1 Thursday

Ribwort plantain, *Plantago lanceolata (left)*; Russian comfrey, *Symphytum × uplandicum* (II); broom, *Cytisus scoparius* (III); and ribbed melilot, *Melilotus officinalis* (IV)

JUNE *1995*

5 Monday

HOLIDAY, REPUBLIC OF IRELAND
HOLIDAY, NEW ZEALAND (QUEEN'S BIRTHDAY)

6 Tuesday ◑

7 Wednesday

8 Thursday

9 Friday

10 Saturday

11 Sunday

TRINITY SUNDAY

Bullace, *Prunus domestica* ssp. *insititia* (opposite) and a
cultivar of apple, *Malus domestica* (right)

12 Monday

16 Friday

13 Tuesday ○

17 Saturday

14 Wednesday

18 Sunday   FATHER'S DAY, UK, CANADA AND USA

15 Thursday   CORPUS CHRISTI

Common dog violet, *Viola riviniana* (I); opposite-leaved golden saxifrage, *Chrysosplenium oppositifolium* (II); bulbous buttercup, *Ranunculus bulbosus* (III); ivy-leaved toadflax, *Cymbalaria muralis* (IV); hoary willowherb, *Epilobium parviflorum* (V); white melilot, *Melilotus alba* (VI); and hoary plantain, *Plantago media* (VII)

XV. Pale Wood Violet.
Viola Sylvestris.
Tunbridge Wells.
May 11. 1901.

I.

IV. Ivy-leaved Toad-flax.
(Mother-of-Thousands.)
Linaria Cymbalaria.

Old wall, close to Spa Hotel.
Tunbridge Wells.

May 8. 1901.

IV.)

III. Bulbous Buttercup.
Ranunculus bulbosus.
Molyneux Park. meadow.
Tunbridge Wells.
May. 13. 1901.

III.

VI.

VII. Hoary Plantain. Lamb's-tongue.
Plantago media.
Chelsfield lane. August 5. 1901.

II.

II. Common Golden Saxifrage.
Chrysosplenium oppositifolium.

Marsh.
Tunbridge Wells.
May 11. 1901.

V.)

V. Small-flowered Hairy Willow-Herb.
Epilobium parviflorum.
Tunbridge Wells.
Bank of stream.
July 11. 1901.

VI. White Melilot. Melilotus alba.
Derry Downs. St Mary Cray.
August 6. 1901.

VII.

I. Field Wood-Rush.
Juncoides Campestre.

May. 10. 1901.

Pasture.
Tunbridge Wells.

I.

II. Yellow Dead-nettle, Weasel-snout, Archangel.
Lamium Galeöbdolun.

Speldhurst Wood.
May 15. 1901.

II.

III. Large-flowered Bitter-Cress.
Cardamine amara.

Tunbridge Wells.
Riverside near Hurst Wood.

June 5. 1901.

III)

V.

IV.

V.

Ox-eye Daisy. Chrysanthemum leucanthemum.

Tunbridge Wells. Meadows.

June 26. 1901.

IV.

Common Sainfoin, Cock's-head.
Onobrychis viciæfolia.
Ramsgate. June 11. 1901.

19 Monday ◑

23 Friday

20 Tuesday   RHS FLOWER SHOW

24 Saturday

21 Wednesday   SUMMER SOLSTICE
                              RHS FLOWER SHOW

25 Sunday

22 Thursday

Field wood-rush, *Luzula campestris* (I); yellow archangel, *Lamium galeobdolon* (II); large bittercress, *Cardamine amara* (III); sainfoin, *Onobrychis viciifolia* (IV); and
ox-eye daisy, *Leucanthemum vulgare* (V)

JUNE/JULY *1995*

26 Monday

27 Tuesday

28 Wednesday ●

29 Thursday

30 Friday

1 Saturday   CANADA DAY

2 Sunday

Greater celandine, *Chelidonium majus* (I); common twayblade, *Listera ovata* (II); rosebay willowherb, *Epilobium angustifolium* (III); small scabious, *Scabiosa columbaria* (IV); and white mullein, *Verbascum lychnitis* (V)

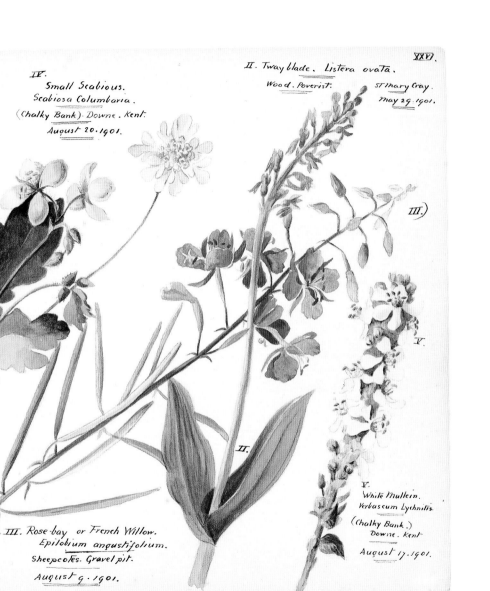

I.
Greater Celandine.
Chelidonium Major

Tunbridge Wells. Hedge.
May 10. 1901.

IV.
Small Scabious.
Scabiosa Columbaria.
(Chalky Bank). Downe. Kent.
August 20. 1901.

II. Twayblade. Listera ovata.

Wood. Poverist.   St Mary Cray.
                         May 29. 1901.

I.

IV.

III.)

V.

II.

III. Rose-bay or French Willow.
Epilobium angustifolium.
Sheepcotes. Gravel pit.

August 9. 1901.

V.
White Mullein.
Verbascum Lychnitis.
(Chalky Bank.)
Downe. Kent

August 17. 1901.

I. Hairy Tare.
Vicia hirsuta.

Hedge. Bishop's Down.
Tunbridge Wells.
May 20. 1901.

I.

Small Marsh Valerian.
Valeriana dioica.

Marshy ground.
Speldhurst Wood.
May 18. 1901.

II.

III.
Broad-leaved Garlic.
(Ransoms.)
Allium ursinum.

Wood near Tunbridge Wells.
May 20. 1901.

III.

IV. Wood Strawberry.
Fragaria Vesca
Speldhurst. (Bank.)
May 20. 1901.

V.

V. Mountain Speedwell.
Veronica montana.

Moist meadows and woods.
Speldhurst. Tunbridge Wells.
May 22. 1901.

JULY *1995*

3 Monday   HOLIDAY, CANADA (CANADA DAY)

7 Friday   HAMPTON COURT PALACE FLOWER SHOW

4 Tuesday   HOLIDAY, USA (INDEPENDENCE DAY)

8 Saturday   HAMPTON COURT PALACE FLOWER SHOW

5 Wednesday ◑   HAMPTON COURT PALACE FLOWER SHOW

9 Sunday   HAMPTON COURT PALACE FLOWER SHOW

6 Thursday   HAMPTON COURT PALACE FLOWER SHOW

Hairy tare, *Vicia hirsuta* (I); common valerian, *Valeriana officinalis* (II); ramsons or wild garlic, *Allium ursinum* (III); wild strawberry, *Fragaria vesca* (IV); and wood speed-well, *Veronica montana* (V)

JULY *1995*

10 Monday

---

11 Tuesday

---

12 Wednesday ○   HOLIDAY, N. IRELAND
(BATTLE OF THE BOYNE)

---

13 Thursday

14 Friday

15 Saturday   ST. SWITHIN'S DAY

16 Sunday

Hop trefoil, *Trifolium campestre* (opposite) and common
milkwort, *Polygala vulgaris* (right)

JULY *1995*

17 Monday

18 Tuesday   RHS FLOWER SHOW

19 Wednesday ☽   RHS FLOWER SHOW

20 Thursday

21 Friday

22 Saturday

23 Sunday

Wood spurge, *Euphorbia amygdaloides* (I); early purple orchid, *Orchis mascula* (II); musk or nodding thistle, *Carduus nutans* (III); common marsh bedstraw, *Galium palustre* (IV); and cross-leaved heath, *Erica tetralix* (V)

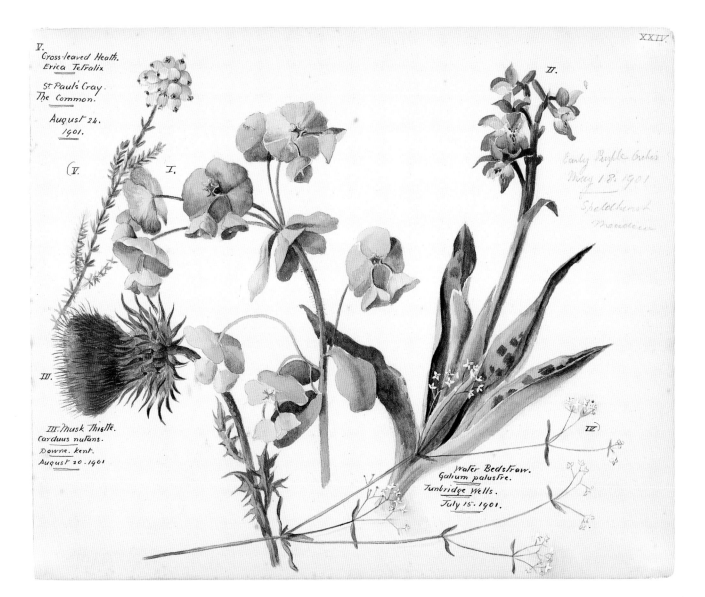

V.
Cross-leaved Heath.
Erica Tetralix

St Paul's Cray.
The Common.

August 24.
1901.

Ⅴ.

Ⅰ.

Ⅱ.

Early Purple Orchis
May 18. 1901

"Spotchhurst
Meadow"

Ⅲ.

Ⅲ. Musk Thistle.
Carduus nutans.
Downe. Kent.
August 20. 1901

Ⅳ.

Water Bedstraw.
Galium palustre.
Tunbridge Wells.
July 15. 1901.

I.
Mealy Guelder Rose. Wayfaring Tree.
Viburnum Lantana.

May 20. 1901.

St Mary Cray

II. Lesser Spearwort.
Ranunculus Flammula.

Moist Meadow.
Speldhurst. Tun. Wells.

June 1. 1901.

II.

IV.
Ground Thistle.
Cnicus acaulis.

Chalky meadow near East Hall. St Mary Cray

August 6. 1901.

I.

III.

IV.

III.
Common Yellow Cow-wheat.
Melampyrum Pratense.

Hurst Wood.
Tunbridge Wells.

June 1. 1901.

24 Monday

28 Friday

25 Tuesday

29 Saturday

26 Wednesday

30 Sunday

27 Thursday ●

Wayfaring tree, *Viburnum lantana* (I); lesser spearwort, *Ranunculus flammula* (II); common cow-wheat, *Malampyrum pratense* (III); and dwarf or ground thistle, *Cirsium acaule* (IV)

JULY/AUGUST *1995*

31 Monday

1 Tuesday

2 Wednesday

3 Thursday

4 Friday ◑

5 Saturday

6 Sunday

Dusky crane's-bill, *Geranium phaeum* (I); globeflower or witches' gowan, *Trollius europaeus* (II); bird cherry, *Prunus padus* (III); celery-leaved buttercup, *Ranunculus sceleratus* (IV); red clover, *Trifolium pratense* (V); and cathartic flax, *Linum catharticum* (VI)

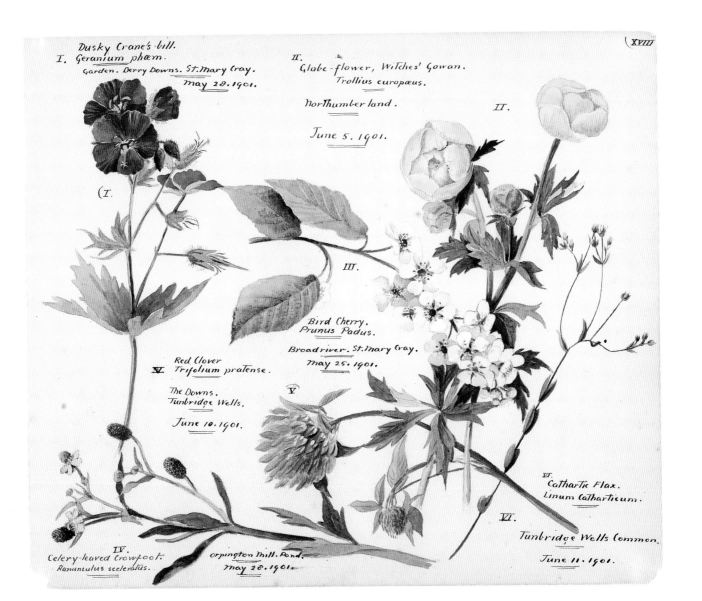

Dusky Crane's-bill.
I. Geranium phæm.
Garden. Derry Downs. St. Mary Cray.
May 28. 1901.

II. Globe-flower, Witches' Gowan.
Trollius europæus.

Northumberland.

June 5. 1901.

II.

(I.)

III.

Bird Cherry.
Prunus Padus.

Broadriver. St. Mary Cray.
May 25. 1901.

V. Red Clover
Trifolium pratense.

The Downs.
Tunbridge Wells.

June 10. 1901.

V.

VI. Cathartic Flax.
Linum Catharticum.

VI.

IV. Celery-leaved Crowfoot.
Ranunculus sceleratus.

Orpington Mill Pond.
May 28. 1901.

Tunbridge Wells Common.

June 11. 1901.

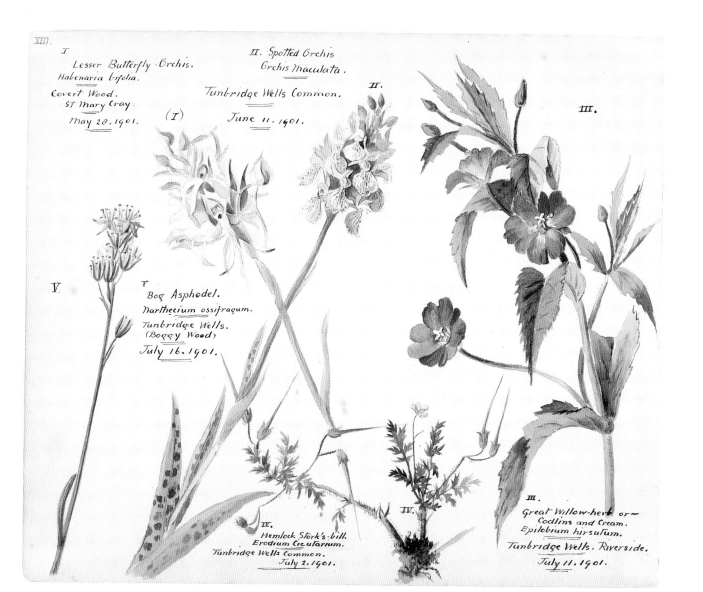

I.
Lesser Butterfly-Orchis.
Habenaria bifolia.
Covert Wood.
St Mary Cray.
May 28. 1901.

(I)

II. Spotted Orchis
Orchis maculata.
II.
Tunbridge Wells Common.
June 11. 1901.

III.

V
Bog Asphodel.
Narthecium ossifragum.
Tunbridge Wells.
(Boggy Wood)
July 16. 1901.

V.

IV.
Hemlock Stork's-bill.
Erodium cicutarium.
Tunbridge Wells Common.
July 2. 1901.

IV.

III.
Great Willow-herb or —
Codlins and Cream.
Epilobium hirsutum.
Tunbridge Wells. Riverside.
July 11. 1901.

AUGUST *1995*

7 Monday   SUMMER HOLIDAY, SCOTLAND
HOLIDAY, REPUBLIC OF IRELAND

11 Friday

8 Tuesday

12 Saturday   WISLEY FLOWER SHOW

9 Wednesday

13 Sunday   WISLEY FLOWER SHOW

10 Thursday ○

Greater butterfly orchid, *Platanthera chlorantha* (I); heath spotted orchid, *Dactylorhiza maculata* (II); greater willowherb, *Epilobium hirsutum* (III); common stork's bill, *Erodium cicutarium* (IV); and bog asphodel, *Narthecium ossifragum* (V)

AUGUST *1995*

14 Monday

15 Tuesday   RHS FLOWER SHOW

16 Wednesday   RHS FLOWER SHOW

17 Thursday

18 Friday ◐

19 Saturday

20 Sunday

Probably shasta daisy (a frequent garden escape through-
out England), *Leucanthemum* x *superbum* (opposite) and
great burnet, *Sanguisorba officinalis* (right)

AUGUST *1995*

21 Monday

22 Tuesday

23 Wednesday

24 Thursday

25 Friday

26 Saturday ●

27 Sunday

Yellow iris, *Iris pseudacorus* (I); marsh cudweed, *Gnaphalium uliginosum* (II); barberry, *Berberis vulgaris* (III); skullcap, *Scutellaria galericulata* (IV); and enchanter's nightshade, *Circaea lutetiana* (below)

I. Corn Flag, Yellow Iris.
Iris Pseudacorus.

Side of stream.
Southover. Burwash.

June 17. 1901.

Gnaphalium
Cud-weed. June 29. 1901.
Tunbridge Wells.

III. Barberry.
Berberis vulgaris.

Tunbridge Wells. Hedge.
Nr. Broadwater
June 19. 1901.

III)

I.

II

IV.

IV. Greater Skull-cap.
Scutellaria galericulata.

Southover. Burwash.
(Bank of Pond.)

July 8. 1901.

Enchanter's Nightshade.
Circæa lutetiana.
Orpington Mill.
August 20. 1901.

I. Jagged-leaved Crane's-bill.
Geranium dissectum.
Meadow. Molyneux Park.
Tun. Wells.
June 18. 1901.

II. Buttercup.
Ranunculus acris.
Meadow. Rusthall.
June 22. 1901.

IV.ᴬ Evening Campion.
Lychnis alba.
Well Hill. Chelsfield.
August 7. 1901.

III.

II.

III.

Orpington Mill.
August 4. 1901.

IV.ᴮ Evening Campion.
Lychnis alba. (Red variety.)
Wood. St Mary Cray.
August 31. 1901.

AUGUST/SEPTEMBER *1995*

28 Monday   SUMMER HOLIDAY, UK (EXC. SCOTLAND)

29 Tuesday

30 Wednesday

31 Thursday

1 Friday

2 Saturday ◑

3 Sunday

Cut-leaved crane's-bill, *Geranium dissectum* (I); meadow buttercup, *Ranunculus acris* (II); field pansy, *Viola arvensis* (III); white campion, *Silene latifolia* (IVA); and red campion, *Silene dioica* (IVB)

SEPTEMBER *1995*

4 Monday   HOLIDAY, CANADA (LABOUR DAY)
AND USA (LABOR DAY)

8 Friday

5 Tuesday

9 Saturday ○

6 Wednesday

10 Sunday

7 Thursday

Marsh thistle, *Cirsium palustre* (I); small-flowered crane's-bill, *Geranium pusillum* (II); probably side-flowering shoot of nettle-leaved bellflower, *Campanula trachelium* (III); kidney vetch, *Anthyllis vulneraria* (IV); and white bryony, *Bryonia dioica* (below right)

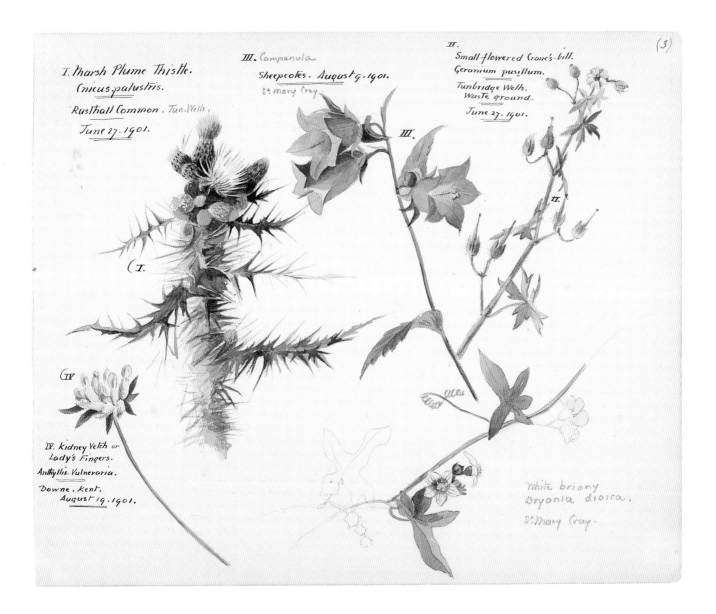

I. Marsh Plume Thistle.
Cnicus palustris.

Rusthall Common. Tun. Wells.
June 27. 1901.

III. Campanula
Sheepcotes. August 9. 1901.
St mary Cray.

II. Small-flowered Crane's-bill.
Geranium pusillum.
Tunbridge Wells.
Waste ground.
June 27. 1901.

III.

(I.

II.

IV

IV. Kidney Vetch or
Lady's Fingers.
Anthyllis. Vulneraria.
Downe. Kent.
August 19. 1901.

White briony
Bryonia dioica.
St Mary Cray.

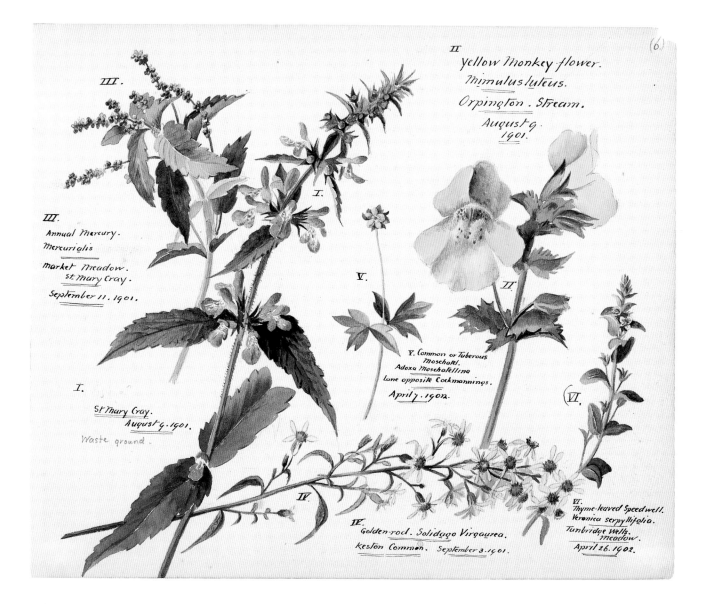

(6.)

III.

II
Yellow Monkey flower.
Mimulus luteus.
Orpington. Stream.
August 9.
1901.

III.
Annual Mercury.
Mercurialis
Market Meadow.
St. Mary Cray.
September 11. 1901.

I.

II.

V.

V. Common or Tuberous
Moschatel.
Adoxa Moschatellina.
Lane opposite Cockmannings.
April 7. 1902.

I.
St. Mary Cray.
August 9. 1901.
Waste ground.

(VI.)

IV.

IV.
Golden-rod. Solidago Virgaurea.
Keston Common.   September 3. 1901.

VI. Thyme-leaved Speedwell.
Veronica serpyllifolia.
Tunbridge Wells.
Meadow.
April 26. 1902.

11 Monday

15 Friday HARROGATE GREAT AUTUMN SHOW

12 Tuesday RHS GREAT AUTUMN SHOW

16 Saturday ◗ HARROGATE GREAT AUTUMN SHOW

13 Wednesday RHS GREAT AUTUMN SHOW

17 Sunday

14 Thursday

Probably woundwort, *Stachys × ambigua* (I); monkey flower, *Mimulus guttatus* (II); annual mercury, *Mercuralis annua* (III); goldenrod, *Solidago virgaurea* (IV); moschatel or townhall clock, *Adoxa moschatellina* (V); and thyme-leaved speedwell, *Veronica serpyllifolia* (VI)

SEPTEMBER *1995*

18 Monday

19 Tuesday

20 Wednesday

21 Thursday

22 Friday

23 Saturday   AUTUMNAL EQUINOX

24 Sunday ●

Yellow-wort, *Blackstonia perfoliata* (opposite) and creeping Jenny, *Lysimachia nummularia* (right)

25 Monday   JEWISH NEW YEAR (ROSH HASHANAH)

26 Tuesday

27 Wednesday

28 Thursday

29 Friday   MICHAELMAS DAY

30 Saturday

1 Sunday ◑

Long-stalked crane's-bill, *Geranium columbinum* (I); hemp agrimony, *Eupatorium cannabinum* (II); devilsbit scabious, *Succisa pratensis* (III); silverweed, *Potentilla anserina* (IV); and lesser skullcap, *Scutellaria minor* (V)

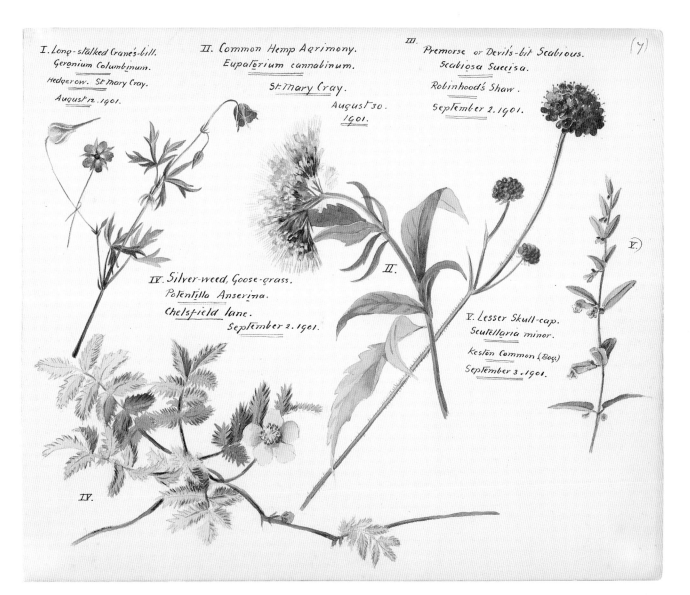

I. Long-stalked Crane's-bill.
Geranium Columbinum.

Hedgerow. St Mary Cray.

August 12. 1901.

II. Common Hemp Agrimony.
Eupatorium cannabinum.

St Mary Cray.

August 30.
1901.

III.
Premorse or Devil's-bit Scabious.
Scabiosa Succisa.

Robinhood's Shaw.

September 2. 1901.

(7)

II.

IV. Silver-weed, Goose-grass.
Potentilla Anserina.

Chelsfield lane.
September 2. 1901.

V.)

V. Lesser Skull-cap.
Scutellaria minor.

Keston Common (Bog.)
September 3. 1901.

IV.

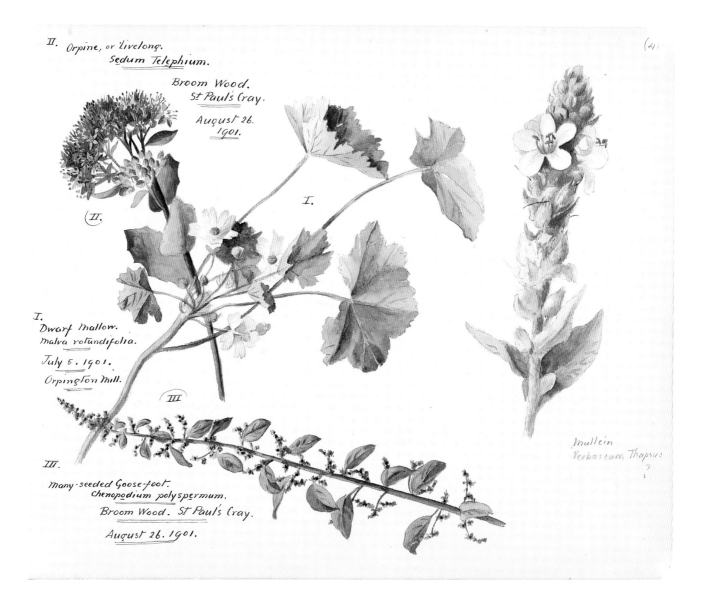

II. Orpine, or livelong.
    Sedum Telephium.

Broom Wood.
St Paul's Cray.

August 26.
1901.

II.

I.

(41)

I.
Dwarf Mallow.
Malva rotundifolia.

July 5. 1901.

Orpington Mill.

III.

III.

Many-seeded Goose-foot.
    Chenopodium polyspermum.

Broom Wood. St Paul's Cray.

August 26. 1901.

Mullein
Verbascum Thapsus
?

2 Monday

6 Friday

3 Tuesday   RHS FLOWER SHOW

7 Saturday

4 Wednesday   JEWISH DAY OF ATONEMENT (YOM KIPPUR)
RHS FLOWER SHOW

8 Sunday ○

5 Thursday

Dwarf mallow, *Malva neglecta* (I); orpine, *Sedum tele-phium* (II); many-seeded goosefoot or allseed, *Chenopodium polyspermum* (III); and great mullein or Aaron's rod, *Verbascum thapsus* (right)

OCTOBER *1995*

9 Monday

JEWISH FESTIVAL OF TABERNACLES
(SUCCOTH) FIRST DAY
HOLIDAY, CANADA (THANKSGIVING)
AND USA (COLUMBUS DAY)

10 Tuesday

11 Wednesday

12 Thursday

13 Friday

14 Saturday

15 Sunday

Red hemp-nettle, *Galeopsis angustifolia* (I); upright hedge-parsley, *Torilis japonica* (I); common dodder, *Cuscuta epithymum* (III); and polyanthus, *Primula × polyantha* (IV)

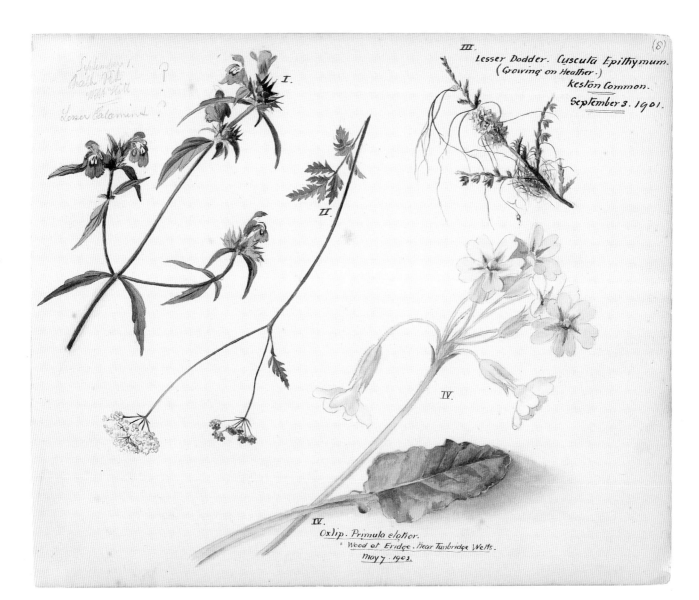

I.

II.

III.

Lesser Dodder. Cuscuta Epithymum.
(Growing on Heather.)
Keston Common.
September 3. 1901.

IV.

IV.
Oxlip. Primula elatior.
Wood at Eridge. Near Tunbridge Wells.
May 7. 1901.

September 1.
Bath Net
Hill Hill
Lesser Calamint ?

(8)

(9)

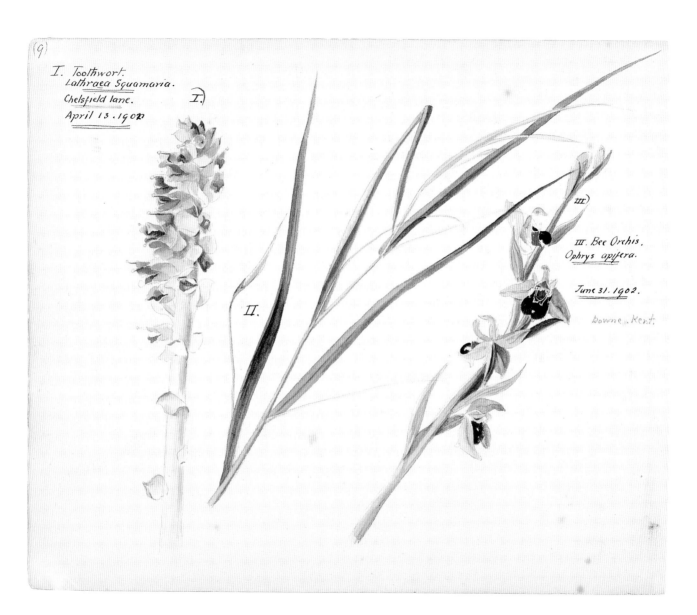

I. Toothwort.
Lathraea Squamaria.
Chelsfield lane.
April 13. 1902

I.)

II.

III.)

III. Bee Orchis.
Ophrys apifera.

June 31. 1902.

Downe, Kent.

16 Monday ◑   JEWISH FESTIVAL OF TABERNACLES
(SUCCOTH) EIGHTH DAY

20 Friday

17 Tuesday

21 Saturday

18 Wednesday

22 Sunday   BRITISH SUMMER TIME ENDS
(SUBJECT TO CONFIRMATION)

19 Thursday

Toothwort, *Lathraea squamaria* (I); grass vetchling, *Lathyrus nissolia* (II); and bee orchid, *Ophrys apifera* (III)

OCTOBER *1995*

23 Monday   HOLIDAY, NEW ZEALAND (LABOUR DAY)

24 Tuesday ●   UNITED NATIONS DAY

25 Wednesday

26 Thursday

27 Friday

28 Saturday

29 Sunday

Narrow-leaved bird's-foot trefoil, *Lotus glaber* (opposite)
and cow basil, *Vaccaria hispanica* (right)

OCTOBER/NOVEMBER *1995*

30 Monday ◑   HOLIDAY, REPUBLIC OF IRELAND

3 Friday

31 Tuesday   HALLOWE'EN
RHS FLOWER SHOW

4 Saturday

1 Wednesday   ALL SAINTS' DAY
RHS FLOWER SHOW

5 Sunday   GUY FAWKES' DAY, UK

2 Thursday

Petty whin or needle furze, *Genista anglica* (I); purple
loosestrife, *Lythrum salicaria* (II); and tuberous comfrey,
Symphytum tuberosum (III)

I.

I.
Petty or Needle Whin.
Genista anglica.

Broadwater Forest.
Tunbridge Wells.
June 2. 1902.

III.

III. Common Comfrey.
Symphytum officinale
Tunbridge Wells.
June 6. 1902.

II.

II. Purple Loosestrife.
Lythrum Salicaria.
Eynsford.
(marshy ground.)
August 12. 1904.

12.

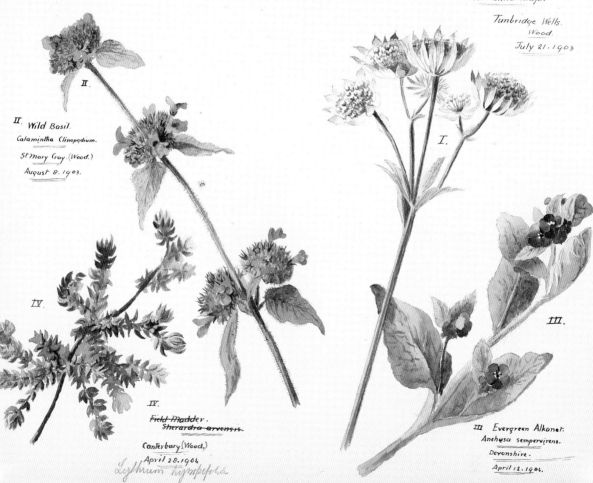

I. Greater Astrantia.
Astrantia major

Tunbridge Wells.
Wood.
July 21. 1903

II. Wild Basil.
Calamintha Clinopodium.

St Mary Cray. (Wood.)

August 8. 1903.

II.

I.

IV.

IV.

Field Madder.
Sherardia arvensis.

Canterbury (Wood.)

April 28. 1904.

Lythrum hyssopifolia

III.

III. Evergreen Alkanet.
Anchusa sempervirens.

Devonshire.

April 12. 1904.

6 Monday

10 Friday   HOLIDAY, USA (VETERANS' DAY)

7 Tuesday ○

11 Saturday   VETERANS' DAY, USA
HOLIDAY, CANADA (REMEMBRANCE DAY)

8 Wednesday

12 Sunday   REMEMBRANCE SUNDAY

9 Thursday

Great masterwort, *Astrantia major* (I); wild basil, *Clinopodium vulgare* (II); green alkanet, *Pentaglottis sempervirens* (III); and field madder, *Sherardia arvensis* (IV)

NOVEMBER *1995*

13 Monday

17 Friday

14 Tuesday

18 Saturday

15 Wednesday ◐

19 Sunday

16 Thursday

Small toadflax, *Chaenorhinum minus* (I); yellow water-lily, *Nuphar lutea* (centre); and reversed clover, *Trifolium resupinatum* (III)

14.

I
Least Toad-flax.
Linaria viscida.
St Mary Cray.
Wood.
August 6. 1903.

I.

III.

Teaz

Mangel-leaved T.
T. Squamosum
June 24th 1905.

I. Galeopsis Tetrahit.
Common Hempnettle.
August 9. 1903.
St Mary Cray. Edge of Wood.

I.

II. Red Bartsia.
Bartsia Odontites.
Chelsfield. Wood.
August 8. 1903.

20 Monday

24 Friday

21 Tuesday   RHS FLOWER SHOW

25 Saturday

22 Wednesday ●   RHS FLOWER SHOW

26 Sunday

23 Thursday   HOLIDAY, USA (THANKSGIVING DAY)

Common hemp-nettle, *Galeopsis tetrahit* (I); and red
bartsia, *Odontites vernus* (II)

NOVEMBER *1995*

27 Monday

---

28 Tuesday

---

29 Wednesday ◑

---

30 Thursday   ST. ANDREW'S DAY, SCOTLAND

DECEMBER *1995*

1 Friday

2 Saturday

3 Sunday   ADVENT SUNDAY

Whorled clary, *Salvia verticillata* (opposite) and viper's
bugloss, *Echium vulgare* (right)

DECEMBER *1995*

4 Monday

5 Tuesday

6 Wednesday

7 Thursday ○

8 Friday

9 Saturday

10 Sunday

Common water crowfoot, *Ranunculus aquatilis* (1); and
common figwort, *Scrophularia nodosa* (below)

13.)

I.

Water Crowfoot.
Ranunculus aquatilis.

Rusthall Common.
(Pond)
May 25. 1904.

I.

Shade Figwort.
Scrophularia.
S. umbrosa.

(1)

Shepherd's Needle, Venus' Comb,
Scandix Pecten Veneris.

Tunbridge Wells.

June 10th. 1905.

I

II Water
Mountain Avens.

Topley Ryke.
Buxton.
July 27. 1905.

II

III.

III.

Buxton. (Grinlow Tower.)
July 31. 1905.

DECEMBER *1995*

11 Monday

15 Friday ◐

12 Tuesday   RHS CHRISTMAS SHOW

16 Saturday

13 Wednesday   RHS CHRISTMAS SHOW

17 Sunday

14 Thursday

Shepherd's needle, *Scandix pecten-veneris* (I); water avens, *Geum rivale* (II); and mountain pansy, *Viola lutea* (III)

DECEMBER *1995*

18 Monday   CHANUKAH, FIRST DAY

19 Tuesday

20 Wednesday

21 Thursday

22 Friday ●   WINTER SOLSTICE

23 Saturday

24 Sunday   CHRISTMAS EVE

Heath speedwell, *Veronica officinalis* (1); germander speedwell, *Veronica chamaedrys* (2); and wood speedwell, *Veronica montana* (3)

Scrophularinæ

(2) Germander Speedwell, Blue Speedwell,
Bird's-eye.
V. chamædrys.

(I.) Common Speedwell. V. officinalis.

(3) Mountain Speedwell.
V. montana.

I.

(2)

(3)

DECEMBER *1995*

25 Monday

CHRISTMAS DAY
CHANUKAH, EIGHTH DAY

26 Tuesday

BOXING DAY, ST. STEPHEN'S DAY
HOLIDAY (EXC. USA)

27 Wednesday

28 Thursday ◑

29 Friday

30 Saturday

31 Sunday

Wild radish, *Raphanus raphanistrum* (opposite) and
hound's tongue, *Cynoglossum officinale* (right)

EUROPEAN NATIONAL HOLIDAYS 1995

Holidays that fall on a Sunday are not included

Austria	January 6; April 17; May 1, 25; June 5, 15; August 15; October 26; November 1; December 8, 25, 26
Belgium	April 17; May 1, 25; June 5, 21; August 15; November 1, 11; December 25
Denmark	April 13, 14, 17; May 12, 25; June 5; December 25, 26
France	April 17; May 1, 8, 25; June 5; July 14; August 15; November 1; December 25
Germany	April 14, 17; May 1, 25; June 5; October 3; November 22; December 25, 26
Italy	January 6; April 17, 25; May 1; August 15; November 1; December 8, 25, 26
Luxembourg	April 17; May 1, 25; June 5, 23; August 15; November 1, 2; December 25, 26
Netherlands	April 17; May 5, 25; June 5; December 25, 26
Norway	April 13, 14, 17; May 1, 17, 25; June 5; December 25, 26
Portugal	April 25; May 1; June 10, 15; August 15; October 5; November 1; December 1, 8
Spain	January 6; April 14; May 1; August 15; October 12; November 1; December 6, 8, 25
Sweden	January 6; April 14, 17; May 1, 25; June 5, 24; November 4; December 25, 26
Switzerland	April 14, 17; May 1, 25; June 5; August 1; December 25, 26